What is the Church?

Pope Francis

GW00686367

*All booklets are published thanks to the
generous support of the members of the
Catholic Truth Society*

CATHOLIC TRUTH SOCIETY

PUBLISHERS TO THE HOLY SEE

Contents

ISBN 978 1 86082 919 2

Introduction

The Holy Spirit, life of the Church

In the Creed, immediately after professing our faith in the Holy Spirit, we say: "I believe in one, holy, catholic and apostolic Church". There is a profound connection between these two realities of faith: indeed it is the Holy Spirit who gives life to the Church, who guides her steps. Without the constant presence and action of the Holy Spirit the Church could not live and could not carry out the task that the Risen Jesus entrusted to her: to go and make disciples of all nations (cf. *Mt* 28:19).

Evangelising is the Church's mission. It is not the mission of only a few, but it is mine, yours and our mission. The Apostle Paul exclaimed: "Woe to me if I do not preach the Gospel!" (*1 Cor* 9:16). We must all be evangelisers, especially with our life! Paul VI stressed that "Evangelising is...the grace and vocation proper to the Church, her deepest identity. She exists in order to evangelise" (Apostolic Exhortation, *Evangelii Nuntiandi*, n. 14).

The "driving force" of evangelisation

Who is the real driving force of evangelisation in our life and in the Church? Paul VI wrote clearly:

"it is the Holy Spirit who today, just as at the beginning of the Church, acts in every evangeliser who allows himself to be possessed and led by him. The Holy Spirit places on his lips the words which he could not find by himself, and at the same time the Holy Spirit predisposes the soul of the hearer to be open and receptive to the Good News and to the Kingdom being proclaimed" (*ibid*., n. 75).

To evangelise, therefore, it is necessary to open ourselves once again to the horizon of God's Spirit, without being afraid of what he asks us or of where he leads us. Let us entrust ourselves to him! He will enable us to live out and bear witness to our faith, and will illuminate the heart of those we meet.

The transformer of our hearts

This was the experience at Pentecost. "There appeared" to the Apostles gathered in the Upper Room with Mary, "tongues as of fire, distributed and resting on each one of them. And they were all filled with the Holy Spirit and began to speak in other tongues, as the Spirit gave them utterance" (*Ac* 2:3-4). In coming down upon the Apostles the Holy Spirit makes them leave the room they had locked themselves into out of fear, he prompts them to step out of themselves and transforms them into heralds and witnesses of the "mighty works of God" (v. 11). Moreover this transformation brought about by the Holy Spirit reverberated in the multitude that had arrived "from every nation under heaven" (v. 5) for each one heard the Apostles' words as if they had been "speaking in his own language" (v. 6).

Unity

This is one of the first important effects of the action of the Holy Spirit who guides and brings to life the proclamation of the Gospel: unity, communion. It was in Babel, according to the Biblical account, that the dispersion of people and the confusion of languages had begun, the results of the act of pride and conceit of man who wanted to build with his efforts alone, without God, "a city, and a tower with its top in the heavens" (*Gn* 11:4). At Pentecost these divisions were overcome. There was no longer conceit with regard to God, nor the closure of some people to others; instead, there was openness to God, there was going out to proclaim his word: a new language, that of love which the Holy Spirit pours out into our hearts (cf. *Rm* 5:5); a language that all can understand and that, once received, can be expressed in every life and every culture. The language of the Spirit, the language of the Gospel, is the language of communion which invites us to get the better of closedness and indifference, division and antagonisation.

Individual responsibility towards unity

We must all ask ourselves: how do I let myself be guided by the Holy Spirit in such a way that my life and my witness of faith is both unity and communion? Do I convey the word of reconciliation and of love, which is the Gospel, to the milieus in which I live? At times it seems that we are repeating today what happened at Babel: division, the incapacity to understand one another, rivalry, envy, egoism. What do I do with my life? Do I create unity around me? Or do I cause division, by gossip, criticism or envy? What do I do? Let us think about this. Spreading the Gospel means that we are the first to proclaim and live the reconciliation, forgiveness, peace, unity and love which the Holy Spirit gives us. Let us remember Jesus's words: "by this all men will know that you are my disciples, if you have love for one another" (*Jn* 13:34-35).

Courage and confidence

A second element is the day of Pentecost. Peter, filled with the Holy Spirit and standing "with the eleven", "lifted up his voice" (*Ac* 2:14) and "confidently" (v. 29), proclaimed the Good News of Jesus, who gave his life for our salvation and whom God raised from the dead. This is another effect of the Holy Spirit's action: the courage to proclaim the newness of the Gospel of Jesus to all, confidently, (with *parrhesia*) in a loud voice, in every time and in every place. Today too this happens for the Church and for each one of us: the fire of Pentecost, from the action of the Holy Spirit, releases an ever new energy for mission, new ways in which to proclaim the message of salvation, new courage for evangelising. Let us never close ourselves to this action! Let us live the Gospel humbly and courageously!

The joy of evangelisation

Let us witness to the newness, hope and joy that the Lord brings to life. Let us feel within us "the delightful and comforting joy of evangelising" (Paul VI, Apostolic Exhortation, *Evangelii Nuntiandi*, n, 80). Because evangelising, proclaiming Jesus, gives us joy. Instead, egoism makes us bitter, sad, and depresses us. Evangelising uplifts us. I will only mention a third element, which, however, is particularly important: a new evangelisation, a Church which evangelises, must always start with prayer, with asking, like the Apostles in the Upper Room, for the fire of the Holy Spirit. Only a faithful and intense relationship with God makes it possible to get out of our own closedness and proclaim the Gospel with *parrhesia*. Without prayer our acts are empty, and our proclamation has no soul, it is not inspired by the Spirit.

Letting the Holy Spirit lead

Dear friends, as Benedict XVI said, today the Church "feels the wind of the Holy Spirit who helps us, who shows us the right road; and so, we are on our way, it seems to me, with new enthusiasm, and we thank the Lord" (*Address to the Ordinary Assembly of the Synod of Bishops*, 27 October

2012). Let us renew every day our trust in the Holy Spirit's action, the trust that he acts within us, that he is within us, that he gives us apostolic zeal, peace and joy. Let us allow him to lead us. May we be men and women of prayer who witness to the Gospel with courage, becoming in our world instruments of unity and of communion with God.

The Church as the Family of God

Today I would like to begin some catecheses on the mystery of the Church, a mystery which we all experience and of which we are part. I would like to do so with some concepts that are evident in the texts of the Second Vatican Ecumenical Council. Today the first one is: "The Church as the family of God".

The Parable of the Prodigal Son

In recent months I have more than once mentioned the Parable of the Prodigal Son or, rather, of the Merciful Father (cf. *Lk* 15:11-32). The younger son leaves his father's house, squanders all he has and decides to go home again because he realises he has erred. He no longer considers himself worthy to be a son but thinks he has a chance of being hired as a servant. His father, on the contrary, runs to meet him, embraces him, restores to him his dignity as a son and celebrates. This parable, like others in the Gospel, clearly shows God's design for humanity.

An invitation to family life

What is God's plan? It is to make of us all a single family of his children, in which each person feels that God is close and feels loved by him, as in the Gospel parable, feels the warmth of being God's family. The Church is rooted in this great plan. She is not an organisation established by an agreement between a few people, but - as Pope Benedict XVI has so often reminded us - she is a work of God, born precisely from this loving design which is gradually brought about in history. The Church is born from God's wish to call all people to communion with him, to friendship with him, indeed, to share in his own divine life as his sons and daughters. The very word "Church", from the Greek *ekklesia*, means "convocation": God convokes us, he impels us to come out of our individualism, from our tendency to close ourselves into ourselves, and he calls us to belong to his family.

The wisdom of God's design

Furthermore this call originates in creation itself. God created us so that we might live in a profound relationship of friendship with him, and even when sin broke off this relationship with him, with others and with creation, God did not abandon us. The entire history of salvation is the story of God who seeks out human beings, offers them his love and welcomes them. He called Abraham to be the father of a multitude, he chose the People of Israel to make a covenant that would embrace all peoples, and in the fulness of time, he sent forth his Son so that his plan of love and salvation might be fulfilled in a new and eternal Covenant with the whole of humanity. When we read the Gospels, we see that Jesus gathers round him a small community which receives his word, follows it, shares in his journey, becomes his family, and it is with this community that he prepares and builds his Church.

The Church has her roots in the Cross

So what is the Church born from? She is born from the supreme act of love of the Cross, from the pierced side of Jesus from which flowed blood and water, a symbol of the sacraments of the Eucharist and of Baptism. The lifeblood of God's family, of the Church, is God's love which is actualised in loving him and others, all others, without distinction or reservation. The Church is a family in which we love and are loved. When did the Church manifest herself? We celebrated it two Sundays ago [at Pentecost]; she became manifest when the gift of the Holy Spirit filled the heart of the Apostles and spurred them to go out and begin their journey to proclaim the Gospel, spreading God's love.

"'Christ yes, the Church no'"

Still today some say: "Christ yes, the Church no". Like those who say "I believe in God but not in priests". But it is the Church herself which brings Christ to us and which brings us to God. The Church is the great family of God's children. Of course, she also has human aspects. In those who make up the Church, pastors and faithful, there are shortcomings, imperfections and sins. The Pope has these too - and many of them; but what is beautiful is that when we realise we are sinners we encounter the mercy of God who always forgives. Never forget it: God always pardons and receives us into his love of forgiveness and mercy. Some people say that sin is an offence to God, but also an opportunity to humble oneself so as to realise that there is something else more beautiful: God's mercy. Let us think about this.

Falling in love with the Church

Let us ask ourselves today: how much do I love the Church? Do I pray for her? Do I feel part of the family of the Church? What do I do to ensure that she is a community in which each one feels welcome and understood, feels the mercy and love of God who renews life? Faith is a gift and an act which concern us personally, but God calls us to live with our faith together, as a family, as Church. Let us ask the Lord, in a very special way during this Year of Faith, that our communities, the whole Church, be increasingly true families that live and bring the warmth of God.

The People of God

Today I would like to reflect on another term by which the Second Vatican Council defined the Church: "People of God" (cf. Dogmatic Constitution, *Lumen Gentium,* n. 9; *The Catechism of the Catholic Church*, n. 782). And I do so with several questions for each one of you to reflect on.

We belong to God

What does "People of God" mean? First of all it means that God does not belong in a special way to any one people; for it is he who calls us, convokes us, invites us to be part of his people, and this invitation is addressed to all, without distinction, for the mercy of God "desires all men to be saved" (*1 Tm* 2:4). Jesus does not tell the Apostles or us to form an exclusive group, a group of the elite. Jesus says: go out and make disciples of all people (cf. *Mt* 28:19). St Paul says that in the People of God, in the Church, "there is neither Jew nor Greek...for you are all one in Christ Jesus" (*Ga* 3:28). I would also like to say to anyone who feels far away from God and the Church, to anyone who is timid or indifferent, to those who think they can no longer change: the Lord calls you too to become part in his people and he does this with great respect and love! He invites us to be part of this people, the People of God!

Baptism

How does one become a member of this people? It is not
through physical birth, but through a new birth. In the
Gospel, Jesus tells Nicodemus that he needs to be born
from on high, from water and from the Spirit in order to
enter the Kingdom of God (cf. *Jn* 3:3-5). It is through
Baptism that we are introduced into this people, through
faith in Christ, a gift from God that must be nourished and
cultivated throughout our life. Let us ask ourselves: how
do I make this faith that I received in my Baptism grow?
How do I make this faith that I received and that belongs to
the People of God grow?

The Law of Love

Another question: what is the law of the People of
God? It is the law of love, love for God and love for
neighbour according to the new commandment that the
Lord left to us (cf. *Jn* 13:34). It is a love, however, that
is not sterile sentimentality or something vague, but the
acknowledgment of God as the one Lord of life and, at
the same time, the acceptance of the other as my true
brother, overcoming division, rivalry, misunderstanding,
selfishness; these two things go together. Oh how much
more of the journey do we have to make in order actually
to live the new law - the law of the Holy Spirit who acts
in us, the law of charity, of love! Looking in newspapers
or on television we see so many wars between Christians:

how does this happen? Within the People of God, there are so many wars! How many wars of envy, of jealousy, are waged in neighbourhoods, in the workplace! Even within the family itself, there are so many internal wars! We must ask the Lord to make us correctly understand this law of love. How beautiful it is to love one another as true brothers and sisters. How beautiful! Let's do something today. We may all have likes and dislikes; many of us are perhaps a little angry with someone; then let us say to the Lord: Lord, I am angry with this or that person; I am praying to you for him or her. To pray for those with whom we are angry is a beautiful step towards that law of love. Shall we take it? Let's take it today!

God is stronger than evil

What is this People's mission? It is to bring the hope and salvation of God to the world: to be a sign of the love of God who calls everyone to friendship with him; to be the leaven that makes the dough rise, the salt that gives flavour and preserves from corruption, to be a light that enlightens. Look around us - it is enough to open a newspaper, as I said - we see the presence of evil, the Devil is acting. However, I would like to say out loud: God is stronger! Do you believe this, that God is stronger? Let us say it together, let us say it all together: God is stronger! And do you know why he is stronger? Because he is Lord, the only Lord. And I would like to add that reality, at times dark and marked by evil, can change, if we first bring the light of the Gospel especially through our lives. If in a stadium - say the Olympic stadium in Rome or the San Lorenzo in Buenos Aires - on a dark night, if someone turns on a light, you can barely see it but if the other seventy thousand spectators turn on their own light, the whole stadium shines. Let our lives together be the one light of Christ; together we will carry the light of the Gospel to the whole of reality.

We are destined for joy

What is the destination of this People? Our destination is the Kingdom of God, which God himself inaugurated on this earth and which must be extended until its fulfilment, when Christ, our life, shall appear (cf. *Lumen Gentium*, n. 9). The end then is full communion with the Lord, familiarity with the Lord, entry into his own divine life, where we will live in the joy of his love beyond measure, a full joy.

The doors are wide open

Dear brothers and sisters, being the Church, to be the People of God, in accordance with the Father's great design of love, means to be the leaven of God in this humanity of ours. It means to proclaim and to bring God's salvation to this world of ours, so often led astray, in need of answers that give courage, hope and new vigour for the journey. May the Church be a place of God's mercy and hope, where all feel welcomed, loved, forgiven and encouraged to live according to the good life of the Gospel. And to make others feel welcomed, loved, forgiven and encouraged, the Church must be with doors wide open so that all may enter. And we must go out through these doors and proclaim the Gospel.

The Body of Christ

Today I am pausing to reflect on another expression by which the Second Vatican Council indicates the nature of the Church: body; the Council says that the Church is the Body of Christ (cf. *Lumen Gentium*, n. 7). I would like to start with a text from the Acts of the Apostles that we know well: the conversion of Saul, later called Paul, one of the greatest evangelisers (cf. *Ac* 9:4-5).

"'Why do you persecute me?'"

Saul is a persecutor of Christians, but while he is travelling on the road to the city of Damascus, a light suddenly envelops him, he falls to the ground and hears a voice saying to him: "Saul, Saul, why do you persecute me?" He asks: "Who are you, Lord?", and the voice responds: "I am Jesus whom you are persecuting" (v. 3-5). St Paul's experience speaks to us of how profound the union between us Christians and Christ really is. When Jesus ascended into heaven he did not leave us orphans, but through the gift of the Holy Spirit our union with him became even more intense. The Second Vatican Council says that "by communicating his Spirit, Christ mystically constitutes as his body those brothers of his who are called together from every nation" (*Lumen Gentium*, n. 7).

The reality of the body of Christ

The image of the body helps us to understand this profound bond of Church-Christ, which St Paul developed in a particular way in his First Letter to the Corinthians (cf. Chapter 12). First of all, the body reminds us of a living reality. The Church is not a welfare, cultural or political association but a living body that walks and acts in history. And this body has a head, Jesus, who guides, feeds and supports it. This is a point that I would like to emphasise: if one separates the head from the rest of the body, the whole person cannot survive. It is like this in the Church: we must stay ever more deeply connected with Jesus. But not only that: just as it is important that lifeblood flows through the body in order to live, so must we allow Jesus to work in us, let his Word guide us, his presence in the Eucharist feed us, give us life, his love strengthen our love for our neighbour. And this forever! Forever and ever! Dear brothers and sisters, let us stay united to Jesus, let us trust in him, let us orient our life according to his Gospel, let us be nourished by daily prayer, by listening to the Word of God, by sharing in the sacraments.

United as one body

And here I come to a second aspect of the Church as the Body of Christ. St Paul says that just as the limbs of the human body, although diverse and many, form one body, so have we been baptised by one Spirit into one body (cf. *1 Co* 12:12-13). Consequently, in the Church there is variety and a diversity of roles and functions; there is no flat uniformity, but a wealth of gifts that the Holy Spirit distributes. Yet, there is communion and unity: each one relates to the other and comes together to form a single living body, deeply tied to Christ. Let us remember this well: being part of the Church means being united to Christ and receiving from him the divine life that makes us live as Christians; it means staying united to the Pope and to the bishops who are instruments of unity and communion; and it also means learning to overcome subjectivism and division, to understand each other better, to harmonise the variety and the richness of each person; in a word to love God and the people beside us more, in the family, in the parish, in associations. Body and limb, in order to live, must be united! Unity is superior to conflict, always! Conflicts, if not properly resolved, divide us from each other, separate us from God. Conflict can help us to grow, but it can also divide us.

"Unity is superior to conflict"

Let us not go down the path of division, of fighting among ourselves! All united, all united in our differences, but united, always: this is the way of Jesus. Unity is superior to conflict. Unity is a grace for which we must ask the Lord that he may liberate us from the temptation of division, of conflict between us, of selfishness, of gossip.

How much evil gossip does, how much evil! Never gossip about others, never! So much damage to the Church comes from division among Christians, from biases, from narrow interests. Division among us, but also division among communities: Evangelical Christians, Orthodox Christians, Catholic Christians, why are we divided? We must try to bring about unity.

Actively seeking unity

I will tell you something: today, before leaving home, I spent forty minutes, more or less, half an hour, with an evangelical pastor and we prayed together and sought unity. Because we have to pray together as Catholics and also with other Christians, pray that the Lord gives us the gift of unity, unity among us. But how will we have unity among Christians if we are not capable of it among ourselves, as Catholics? Or in our families? So many families fight and are divided! Seek unity, the unity that builds the Church. Unity comes from Jesus Christ. He sends us the Holy Spirit to create unity. Dear brothers and sisters, let us ask God: help us to be members of the Body of the Church, ever more deeply united to Christ; help us not to cause the Body of the Church to suffer through our conflicts, our divisions, our selfishness. Help us to be living limbs bound one to the other by that unique force, love, which the Holy Spirit pours into our hearts (cf. *Rm* 5:5).

The Temple

Today I would like to mention briefly another image that helps us describe the mystery of the Church: the temple (cf. Second Vatican Ecumenical Council, Dogmatic Constitution on the Church, *Lumen Gentium*, n. 6).

Memorial of the history of God's love

What does the word "temple" make us think of? It makes us think of a building, of a construction. More especially the minds of many turn to the history of the People of Israel recounted in the Old Testament. Solomon's great Temple in Jerusalem was the place for the encounter with God in prayer. Inside the Temple was the Ark of the Covenant, a sign of God's presence among the people; and the Ark contained the Tables of the Law, the manna and Aaron's rod. This was a reminder that God had always been in the history of his People, that he had accompanied it on its journey and had guided its steps. The Temple is a memorial of this history. When we go to the Temple we too must remember this history, each one of us our own history, how Jesus met me, how Jesus walked beside me, how Jesus loves and blesses me.

God's house

It is this that was prefigured in the ancient Temple and brought about in the Church by the power of the Holy Spirit: the Church is "God's house", the place of his presence, where we can find and encounter the Lord; the Church is the Temple in which the Holy Spirit dwells. It is he who gives life to her, who guides and sustains her. Let us ask ourselves: where can we meet God? Where can we enter into communion with him through Christ? Where can we find the light of the Holy Spirit to light up our life? The answer is: in the People of God, among us who are the Church. It is here that we shall encounter Jesus, the Holy Spirit and the Father.

Giving God a house

The ancient Temple was built by human hands. There was a wish "to give God a house", to have a visible sign of his presence among the people. With the Incarnation of the Son of God, Nathan's prophecy to King David was fulfilled (cf. *2 S* 7:1-29): it is not the king, it is not we who "give God a house"; rather it is God himself who "builds his house" in order to come and dwell among us, as St John wrote in his Gospel (cf. 1:14). Christ is the living Temple of the Father, and Christ himself builds his "spiritual house": the Church, not made of material stones but rather of "living stones", which we are. The Apostle Paul said to the Christians of Ephesus: you are "built upon the foundation of the apostles and prophets, Christ Jesus himself being the cornerstone, in whom the whole structure is joined together and grows into a holy temple in the Lord; in whom you also are built...for a dwelling place of God in the Spirit" (*Ep* 2:20-22). This is a beautiful thing! We are the living stones of God's building, profoundly united to Christ who is the keystone and also the one that sustains us. What does this mean? It means that we are the temple, we are the living Church, the living temple, and with us when we are together is also the Holy Spirit, who helps us to grow as Church. We are not alone, for we are the People of God: this is the Church!

The divine architect

And it is the Holy Spirit with his gifts who designs the variety. This is important: what does the Holy Spirit do among us? He designs the variety which is a wealth in the Church and unites us, each and every one, to constitute a spiritual temple in which we do not offer material sacrifices but ourselves, our life (cf. *1 P* 2:4-5). The Church is not a fabric woven of things and interests; she is the Temple of the Holy Spirit, the Temple in which God works, the Temple in which, with the gift of Baptism, each one of us is a living stone. This tells us that no one in the Church is useless, and if from time to time someone says to someone else: "go home, you are no good", this is not true. For no one is no good in the Church, we are all necessary for building this Temple! No one is secondary. No one is the most important person in the Church, we are all equal in God's eyes. Some of you might say "Listen, Mr Pope, you are not our equal." Yes, I am like each one of you, we are all equal, we are brothers and sisters! No one is anonymous: we all both constitute and build the Church. This also invites us to reflect on the fact that if the brick of our Christian life goes missing, the beauty of the Church loses something. Some people say, "I have nothing to do with the Church"; but in this way the brick of a life in this beautiful Temple is left out. No one can go away, we must all bring the Church our life, our heart, our love, our thought and our work: all of us together.

Becoming the living stones of the Church

I would now like us to ask ourselves: how do we live our being Church? Are we living stones or are we, as it were, stones that are weary, bored or indifferent? Have you ever noticed how grim it is to see a tired, bored and indifferent Christian? A Christian like that is all wrong, the Christian must be alive, rejoicing in being Christian; he or she must live this beauty of belonging to the People of God which is the Church. Do we open ourselves to the action of the Holy Spirit, to be an active part of our communities or do we withdraw into ourselves, saying, "I have so much to do, it isn't my job!"? The Lord gives all of us his grace, his strength, so that we may be profoundly united to Christ, who is the cornerstone, the pillar and the foundation of our life and of the whole life of the Church. Let us pray that enlivened by his Spirit we may always be living stones of his Church.

The Church Our Mother

Today we resume our catecheses on the Church in this Year of Faith. Among the images that the Second Vatican Council chose to help us understand the nature of the Church better, there is that of "mother": the Church is our mother in faith, in supernatural life (cf. Dogmatic Constitution, *Lumen Gentium*, nn. 6,14,15,41,42). It is one of the images most used by the Fathers of the Church in the first centuries and I think it could be useful for us too. For me it is one of the most beautiful images of the Church: Mother Church! In what sense and in what way is the Church mother? We start with the human reality of motherhood: what makes a mother?

The Church and Our Lady

First of all a mother generates life, she carries her child in her womb for nine months and then delivers him to life, giving birth to him. The Church is like this: she bears us in the faith, through the work of the Holy Spirit who makes her fertile, like the Virgin Mary. The Church and the Virgin Mary are mothers, both of them; what is said of the Church can be said also of Our Lady and what is said of Our Lady can also be said of the Church!

Faith in the family

Certainly faith is a personal act: "I believe", I personally respond to God who makes himself known and wants to enter into friendship with me (cf. *Lumen Fidei*, n. 39). But the faith I receive from others, within a family, within a community that teaches me to say "I believe", "we believe". A Christian is not an island! We do not become Christians in a laboratory, we do not become Christians alone and by our own effort, since the faith is a gift, it is a gift from God given to us in the Church and through the Church. And the Church gives us the life of faith in Baptism: that is the moment in which she gives birth to us as children of God, the moment she gives us the life of God, she engenders us as a mother would.

A vital bond

If you go to the Baptistery of St John Lateran, beside the Pope's Cathedral, inside it there is an inscription in Latin which reads more or less: "Here is born a people of divine lineage, generated by the Holy Spirit who makes these waters life-giving; Mother Church gives birth to her children within these waves". This makes us understand something important: our taking part in the Church is not an exterior or formal fact, it is not filling out a form they give us; it is an interior and vital act; one does not belong to the Church as one belongs to a society, to a party or to any other organisation. The bond is vital, like the bond you have with your mother, because, as St Augustine says, "The Church is truly the mother of Christians" (*De moribus Ecclesiae*, I, 30, 62-63: PL 32, 1336).

Loving the Church as a mother

Let us ask ourselves: how do I see the Church? As I am grateful to my parents for giving me life, am I grateful to the Church for generating me in the faith through Baptism? How many Christians remember the date of their Baptism? I would like to ask you here, but each of you respond in your heart: how many of you remember the date of your Baptism? A few people raise their hands, but many others do not remember! But the date of your Baptism is the day of our birth in the Church, the date on which our mother Church gave us life! And now I leave you with some homework. When you go home today, go and find out what the date of your Baptism is, and then celebrate it, thank the Lord for this gift. Are you going to do it? Do we love the Church as we love our mothers, also taking into account her defects? All mothers have defects, we all have defects, but when we speak of our mother's defects we gloss over them, we love her as she is. And the Church also has her defects: but we love her just as a mother. Do we help her to be more beautiful, more authentic, more in harmony with the Lord? I leave you with these questions, but don't forget your homework: go find the date of your Baptism, carry it in your heart and celebrate it.

The support of a mother

A mother does not stop at just giving life; with great care she helps her children grow, gives them milk, feeds them, teaches them the way of life, accompanies them always with her care, with her affection, with her love, even when they are grown up. And in this she also knows to correct them, to forgive them and understand them. She knows how to be close to them in sickness and in suffering. In a word, a good mother helps her children to come into themselves, and not to remain comfortably under her motherly wings, like a brood of chicks under the wings of the broody hen. The Church like a good mother does the same thing: she accompanies our development by transmitting to us the Word of God, which is a light that directs the path of Christian life; she administers the sacraments. She nourishes us with the Eucharist, she brings us the forgiveness of God through the Sacrament of Penance, she helps us in moments of sickness with the Anointing of the Sick. The Church accompanies us throughout our entire life of faith, throughout the whole of our Christian life. We can then ask ourselves other questions: what is my relationship with the Church? Do I feel like she is my mother who helps me grow as a Christian? Do I participate in the life of the Church, do I feel part of it? Is my relationship a formal or a vital relationship?

A living motherhood

A third brief thought. In the first centuries of the Church, one thing was very clear: the Church, while being the mother of Christians, while "making" Christians, is also "made" by them. The Church is not distinct from us, but should be seen as the totality of believers, as the "we" of Christians: I, you, we all are part of the Church. St Jerome wrote: "The Church of Christ is nothing other than the souls of those who believe in Christ" (Tract. *Ps* 86: PL 26,1084). Thus the motherhood of the Church is lived by us all, pastors and faithful. At times I feel: "I believe in God but not in the Church... I have heard that the Church says... priests say...". Priests are one thing but the Church is not formed solely by priests, the Church is all of us! And if you say that you believe in God and you don't believe in the Church, you are saying that you don't believe in yourself; and this is a contradiction. The Church is all of us: from the baby just baptised to the Bishop, the Pope; we are all the Church and we are all equal in the eyes of God! We are all called to collaborate for the birth of new Christians in the faith, we are all called to be educators in the faith, to proclaim the Gospel. Each of us should ask ourselves: what do I do so that others might share in Christian life? Am I generous in my faith or am I closed? When I repeat that I love a Church that is not closed in herself, but capable of coming out, of moving, even with risks, to bring Christ to all people, I am thinking of everyone, of me, of you, of every Christian! We all take part in the motherhood of the Church, so that the light of Christ may reach the far confines of the earth. Long live Holy Mother Church!

Mother Church Again

Today I am returning to the image of the Church as mother. I am extremely fond of this image of the Church as mother. For this reason I wish to return to it, because I feel that this image not only tells us what the Church is like but also what face the Church - this Mother Church of ours - should increasingly have.

Following what I said last Wednesday I would like to stress three things, still looking at our own mothers, at all they do, at all they experience, at all they suffer for their children. I ask myself: what does a mother do?

Walking beside us

First of all, she teaches how to walk through life, she teaches the right path to take through life, she knows how to guide her children, she always tries to point out to them the right path in life for growing up and becoming adults. And she does so with tenderness, affection, and love, even when she is trying to straighten out our path because we are going a little astray in life or are taking roads that lead to an abyss. A mother knows what's important for a child to enable him to walk the right way through life. Moreover she did not learn it from books but from her own heart. The university of mothers is their heart! They learn there how to bring up their children.

The Church does the same thing: she gives our life direction, she instructs us so that we can follow the right path.

The tenderness of the Ten Commandments

Let us think of the Ten Commandments: they point us to the road to take in order to mature, to anchor our behaviour. They result from the tenderness and from the very love of God who has given them to us. You may say to me: but they are orders! They are a series of 'no's! I would like to ask you to read them - perhaps you have more or less forgotten them - and then think about them in a positive way. You will see that they concern the way we behave to God, to self and to others, exactly what a mother teaches us in order to live correctly. They ask us not to make ourselves material idols that subsequently enslave us. They ask us to remember God, to show our parents respect, to be honest, to respect others... Try to see the commandments in this way and to think of them as though they were the words, the teachings that a mother gives in order to live the best way. A mother never teaches what is evil, she only wants the good of her children and so does the Church.

The defence of a mother

Secondly, I want to tell you: when a child grows up, becomes an adult, he chooses his path, assumes his responsibilities, stands on his own two feet, does what he likes and at times he can also go off course, some accident occurs. A mother has the patience to continue to accompany her children, always and in every situation. It is the force of her love that impels her; a mother can follow her children on their way with discretion and tenderness and, even when they go astray, always finds a way to understand them, to be close, to help. We - in my region - say that a mother can "*dar la cara*". What does this mean? It means that a mother can "stand up for" her children, in other words she is always motivated to defend them. I am thinking of the mothers who suffer for their children in prison or in difficult situations: they do not question whether or not their children are guilty, they keep on loving them. Mothers often suffer humiliation, but they are not afraid, they never cease to give of themselves.

The door is always open

This is how the Church is. She is a merciful mother who understands, who has always sought to help and encourage even those of her children who have erred or are erring; she never closes the door to home. She does not judge but offers God's forgiveness, she offers his love which invites even those of her children who have fallen into a deep abyss to continue on their way. The Church is not afraid to enter their darkness to give them hope; nor is the Church afraid to enter our darkness when we are in the dark night of our soul and our conscience to give us hope! Because the Church is mother!

The intercession of a mother

A last thought: for her children a mother is also able to ask and knock at every door, without calculation; she does so out of love. And I think of how mothers can also and especially knock at the door of God's heart! Mothers say so many prayers for their children, especially for the weaker ones, for those in the greatest need or who have gone down dangerous or erroneous paths in life. A few weeks ago I celebrated Mass in the Church of St Augustine, here in Rome, where the relics of St Monica, his mother, are preserved. How many prayers that holy mother raised to God for her son, and how many tears she shed! I am thinking of you, dear mothers: how often you pray for your children, never tiring! Continue to pray and to entrust them to God; he has a great heart! Knock at God's heart with prayers for your children. The Church does this too: with prayers she puts in the Lord's hands all the situations of her children. Let us trust in the power of the prayer of Mother Church: the Lord is not indifferent. He always knows how to amaze us when we least expect it, as Mother Church knows! These were the thoughts I wanted to share with you today: let us see the Church as a good mother who points out to us the way through life, who is always patient, merciful, understanding and who knows how to put us in God's hands.

The Church is One

In the Creed we say "I believe in one...Church". In other words we profess that the Church is one, and this Church by her nature is one. However if we look at the Catholic Church in the world, we discover that it includes almost three thousand dioceses scattered over all the continents: so many languages, so many cultures! Present here are many bishops from many diverse cultures, from many countries. There is a bishop of Sri Lanka, a bishop of South Africa, a bishop from India, there are many here... bishops from Latin America. The Church is spread throughout the world! And yet the thousands of Catholic communities form a unit. How can this be?

Unity in diversity

We find a concise answer in the *Compendium of the Catechism of the Catholic Church* which says: the Catholic Church in the world "has but one faith, one sacramental life, one apostolic succession, one common hope, and one and the same charity" (n. 161). It is a beautiful definition, clear, it orients us well. Unity in faith, hope and charity, unity in the sacraments, in the ministry: these are like the pillars that hold up and keep together the one great edifice of the Church. Wherever we go, even to the smallest parish in the most remote corner of this earth, there is the one Church. We are at home, we are in the family, we are among brothers and sisters. And this is a great gift of God! The Church is one for us all. There is not one Church for Europeans, one for Africans, one for Americans, one for Asians, one for those who live in Oceania. No, she is one and the same everywhere.

A long distance relationship

It is like being in a family: some of its members may be far away, scattered across the world, but the deep bonds that unite all the members of a family stay solid however great the distance. I am thinking, for example, of my experience of the World Youth Day in Rio de Janeiro: in that endless crowd of young people on the beach at Copacabana we could hear many languages spoken, we could note very different facial features, we came across different cultures and yet there was profound unity, they formed one Church, they were united and one could sense it. Let us all ask ourselves: as a Catholic, do I feel this unity? As a Catholic, do I live this unity of the Church? Or doesn't it concern me because I am closed within my own small group or within myself? Am I one of those who "privatise" the Church to their own group, their own country or their own friends? It is sad to find a "privatised" Church out of selfishness or a lack of faith. It is sad! When I hear that so many Christians in the world are suffering, am I indifferent or is it as if one of my family were suffering? When I think or hear it said that many Christians are persecuted and give their lives for their faith, does this touch my heart or not? Am I open to a brother or sister of the family who is giving his or her life for Jesus Christ? Do we pray for each other?

I have a question for you, but don't answer out loud, only in your heart. How many of you pray for Christians who are being persecuted? How many? Everyone respond in you heart. Do I pray for my brother, for my sister who is in difficulty because they confess and defend their faith? It is important to look beyond our own boundaries, to feel that we are Church, one family in God!

Keeping unity healthy and intact

Let us go a step further and ask ourselves: are there wounds in this unity? Can we hurt this unity? Unfortunately, we see that in the process of history, and now too, we do not always live in unity. At times misunderstanding arises, as well as conflict, tension and division which injure her and so the Church does not have the face we should like her to have; she does not express love, the love that God desires. It is we who create wounds! And if we look at the divisions that still exist among Christians, Catholics, Orthodox, Protestants... we are aware of the effort required to make this unity fully visible. God gives us unity, but we often have a lot of trouble putting it into practice. It is necessary to seek to build communion, to teach communion, to get the better of misunderstandings and divisions, starting with the family, with ecclesial reality, in ecumenical dialogue too. Our world needs unity, this is an age in which we all need unity, we need reconciliation and communion and the Church is the home of communion. St Paul told the Christians of Ephesus: "I therefore, a prisoner for the Lord, beg you to lead a life worthy of the calling to which you have been called, with all lowliness and meekness, with patience, forbearing one another in love, eager to maintain the unity of the Spirit in the bond of peace" (4:1-3).

'Stitching up' the wounds of division

Humility, meekness, magnanimity, love to preserve unity! These, these are the roads, the true roads of the Church. Let us listen to this again. Humility against vanity, against arrogance - humility, meekness, magnanimity, love to preserve unity. Then Paul continued: there is one body, that of Christ that we receive in the Eucharist; and one Spirit, the Holy Spirit who enlivens and constantly recreates the Church; one hope, eternal life; one single faith, one baptism, one God and Father of us all (cf. vv. 4-6). The wealth of what unites us! This is the true wealth: what unites us, not what divides us. This is the wealth of the Church! Let each one ask him- or herself today, "do I increase harmony in my family, in my parish, in my community; or am I a gossip? Am I a cause of division or embarrassment? And you know the harm that gossiping does to the Church, to the parishes, the communities. Gossip does harm! Gossip wounds. Before Christians open their mouths to gossip, they should bite their tongue! To bite one's tongue: this does us good because the tongue swells and can no longer speak, cannot gossip. Am I humble enough to patiently stitch up, through sacrifice, the open wounds in communion?"

The Holy Spirit creates unity

Finally, the last step which takes us to a greater depth. Now, this is a good question: who is the driving force of the Church's unity? It is the Holy Spirit, whom we have all received at Baptism and also in the Sacrament of Confirmation. It is the Holy Spirit. Our unity is not primarily a fruit of our own consensus or of the democracy in the Church, or of our effort to get along with each other; rather, it comes from the One who creates unity in diversity, because the Holy Spirit is harmony and always creates harmony in the Church, and harmonious unity in the many different cultures, languages, and ways of thinking. The Holy Spirit is the mover. This is why prayer is important. It is the soul of our commitment as men and women of communion, of unity. Pray to the Holy Spirit that he may come and create unity in the Church.

Let us ask the Lord: Lord, grant that we be more and more united, never to be instruments of division; enable us to commit ourselves, as the beautiful Franciscan prayer says, to sowing love where there is hatred; where there is injury, pardon; and union where there is discord. So be it.

The Church is Holy

In the Creed, after professing: "I believe in one Church", we add the adjective "holy"; we affirm the sanctity of the Church, and this is a characteristic that has been present from the beginning in the consciousness of early Christians, who were simply called "the holy people" (cf. *Ac* 9:13, 32, 41; *Rm* 8:27; *1 Co* 6:1), because they were certain that it is the action of God the Holy Spirit that sanctifies the Church.

But in what sense is the Church holy if we see that the historical Church, on her long journey through the centuries, has had so many difficulties, problems, dark moments? How can a Church consisting of human beings, of sinners, be holy? Sinful men, sinful women, sinful priests, sinful sisters, sinful bishops, sinful cardinals, a sinful pope? Everyone. How can such a Church be holy?

Christ's love for the Church

To respond to this question I would like to be led by a passage from the Letter of St Paul to the Christians of Ephesus. The Apostle, taking as an example family relationships, states that "Christ loved the Church and gave himself up for her, that he might sanctify her" (5:25-26). Christ loved the Church, by giving himself on the

Cross. And this means that the Church is holy because she comes from God who is holy, he is faithful to her and does not abandon her to the power of death and of evil (cf. *Mt* 16:18). She is holy because Jesus Christ, the Holy One of God (cf. *Mk* 1:24), is indissolubly united to her (cf. *Mt* 28:20). She is holy because she is guided by the Holy Spirit who purifies, transforms, renews. She is not holy by her own merits, but because God makes her holy, it is the fruit of the Holy Spirit and of his gifts. It is not we who make her holy. It is God, the Holy Spirit, who in his love makes the Church holy.

"We are a Church of sinners"

You could say to me: but the Church is made up of sinners, we see them everyday. And this is true: we are a Church of sinners; and we sinners are called to let ourselves be transformed, renewed, sanctified by God. There has been in history the temptation for some to say: the Church is only the Church of the pure, the perfectly consistent, and expels all the rest. This is not true! This is heresy! The Church, that is holy, does not reject sinners; she does not reject us all; she does not reject because she calls everyone, welcomes them, is open even to those furthest from her, she calls everyone to allow themselves to be enfolded by the mercy, the tenderness and the forgiveness of the Father, who offers everyone the possibility of meeting him, of journeying toward sanctity. "Well! Father, I am a sinner, I have tremendous sins, how can I possibly feel part of the Church?" Dear brother, dear sister, this is exactly what the Lord wants, that you say to him: "Lord, here I am, with my sins." Is one of you here without sin? Anyone? No one, not one of us. We all carry our sins with us.

The power of forgiveness

But the Lord wants to hear us say to him: "Forgive me, help me to walk, change my heart!" And the Lord can change your heart. In the Church, the God we encounter is not a merciless judge, but like the father in the Gospel parable. You may be like the son who left home, who sank to the depths, farthest from the Gospel. When you have the strength to say: I want to come home, you will find the door open. God will come to meet you because he is always waiting for you, God is always waiting for you, God embraces you, kisses you and celebrates. That is how the Lord is, that is how the tenderness of our Heavenly Father is.

"A house for everyone"

The Lord wants us to belong to a Church that knows how to open her arms and welcome everyone, that is not a house for the few, but a house for everyone, where all can be renewed, transformed, sanctified by his love, the strongest and the weakest, sinners, the indifferent, those who feel discouraged or lost. The Church offers all the possibility

of following a path of holiness; that is the path of the
Christian. She brings us to encounter Jesus Christ in the
sacraments, especially in Confession and in the Eucharist;
she communicates the Word of God to us, she lets us live
in charity, in the love of God for all. Let us ask ourselves
then, will we let ourselves be sanctified? Are we a Church
that calls and welcomes sinners with open arms, that gives
courage and hope, or are we a Church closed in on herself?
Are we a Church where the love of God dwells, where one
cares for the other, where one prays for the others?

"Do not be afraid of holiness"

A final question: what can I, a weak fragile sinner, do?
God says to you: do not be afraid of holiness, do not be
afraid to aim high, to let yourself be loved and purified by
God, do not be afraid to let yourself be guided by the Holy
Spirit. Let us be infected by the holiness of God. Every
Christian is called to sanctity (cf. Dogmatic Constitution,
Lumen Gentium, nn. 19-42); and sanctity does not consist
especially in doing extraordinary things, but in allowing
God to act. It is the meeting of our weakness with the
strength of his grace, it is having faith in his action that
allows us to live in charity, to do everything with joy and
humility, for the glory of God and as a service to our
neighbour. There is a celebrated saying by the French
writer Léon Bloy, who in the last moments of his life, said:
"The only real sadness in life is not becoming a saint." Let

us not lose the hope of holiness, let us follow this path. Do we want to be saints? The Lord awaits us, with open arms; he waits to accompany us on the path to sanctity. Let us live in the joy of our faith, let us allow ourselves to be loved by the Lord... let us ask for this gift from God in prayer, for ourselves and for others.

The Church is Catholic

"I believe in one, holy, catholic...Church". Today we pause to reflect on this mark of the Church: we say she is catholic, it is the Year of Catholicity. First of all: what does catholic mean? It comes from the Greek "kath'olon" which means "according to the whole", the totality. In what sense does this totality apply to the Church? In what sense do we say the Church is catholic? I would say there are three basic meanings.

The Church as home

The first: the Church is catholic because she is the space, the home in which the faith is proclaimed to us *in its entirety*, in which the salvation brought to us by Christ is offered to everyone. The Church enables us to encounter the mercy of God which transforms us, for in her Jesus Christ is present who has given her the true confession of faith, the fulness of the sacramental life and the authenticity of the ordained ministry. In the Church each one of us finds what is needed to believe, to live as Christians, to become holy and to journey to every place and through every age. To give an example, we can say that it is like family life. In the family, everything that enables us to grow, to mature and to live is given to each of us. We cannot grow up by ourselves, we cannot journey on our own, in isolation; rather, we journey and grow in a community, in a family. And so it is in the Church! In the Church we can listen to the Word of God with the assurance that it is the message that the Lord has given us; in the Church we can encounter the Lord in the sacraments, which are the open windows through which the light of God is given to us, streams from which we can draw God's very life; in the Church we learn to live in the communion and love that comes from God. Each one of us can ask himself or herself today: how do I live in the Church? When I go to church, is it as though I were at the stadium, at a football match? Is it as though I were at the cinema? No, it is something else. How do I go to church? How do I receive the gifts that the Church offers me to grow and mature as a Christian? Do I participate in the life of the community or do I go to church and withdraw into my own problems, isolating myself from others? In this first sense, the Church is catholic because she is everyone's home. Everyone is a child of the Church and in her all find their home.

The Church is universal

A second meaning: the Church is catholic because she is universal, she is spread abroad through every part of the world and she proclaims the Gospel to every man and to every woman. The Church is not a group of elite; she does not only concern the few. The Church has no limits; she is sent to the totality of people, to the totality of the human race. And the one Church is present even in her smallest parts. Everyone can say: in my parish the Catholic Church is present, since it too is part of the universal Church, since it too contains the fulness of Christ's gifts: the faith, the sacraments, the [ordained] ministry; it is in communion with the bishop, with the Pope and it is open to everyone without distinction. The Church does not rest solely beneath the shadow of our steeple; rather, she embraces a vast number of peoples and nations who profess the same faith, are nourished by the same Eucharist, and are served by the same pastors. To feel that we are in communion with the whole Church, with all of the Catholic communities of the world great and small! This is beautiful! And then, to feel we are all on mission, great and small communities alike, that we all must open our doors and go out for the sake of the Gospel. Let us ask ourselves then: what do I do in order to communicate to others the joy of encountering the Lord, the joy of belonging to the Church? Proclaiming and bearing witness to the faith is not the work of the few; it also concerns me, you, each one of us!

The Church as an 'orchestra'

A third and final thought: the Church is catholic, because she is the "home of harmony" where *unity and diversity* know how to merge in order to become a great source of wealth. Let us think about the image of a symphony, which implies accord, harmony, various instruments playing together. Each one preserves its own unmistakable timbre and the sounds characteristic of each blend together around a common theme. Then there is the one who directs it, the conductor, and as the symphony is performed all play together in "harmony", but the timbre of each individual instrument is never eliminated; indeed, the uniqueness of each is greatly enhanced! It is a beautiful image which tells us that the Church is like a great orchestra in which there is great variety. We are not all the same and we do not all have to be the same. We are all different, varied, each of us with his own special qualities. And this is the beauty of the Church: everyone brings his own gift, which God has given him, for the sake of enriching others. And between the various components there is diversity; however, it is a diversity that does not enter into conflict and opposition. It is a variety that allows the Holy Spirit to blend it into harmony. He is the true "Maestro". He is harmony.

Nurturing harmony

And here let us ask ourselves: in our communities do we live in harmony or do we argue amongst ourselves? In my parish community, in my movement, in the place where I am part of the Church, is there gossip? If there is gossip, there is no harmony but rather conflict. And this is not the Church. The Church is everyone in harmony: never gossip about others, never argue! Let us accept others, let us accept that there is a fitting variety, that this person is different, that this person thinks about things in this way or that - that within one and the same faith we can think about things differently - or do we tend to make everything uniform? But uniformity kills life. The life of the Church is variety, and when we want to impose this uniformity on everyone we kill the gifts of the Holy Spirit. Let us pray to the Holy Spirit, who is truly the author of this unity in variety, of this harmony, that he might make us ever more "catholic" in this Church which is catholic and universal!

The Church is Apostolic

When we recite the Creed we say "I believe in one, holy, catholic and apostolic Church". I don't know if you have ever reflected on the meaning of the expression "the Church is apostolic". Perhaps from time to time, coming to Rome, you have thought about the importance of the Apostles Peter and Paul who here gave their lives to bring and bear witness to the Gospel.

The apostolic dimension

But it is even more. To profess that the Church is apostolic means to stress the constitutive bond that she has with the Apostles, with that small group of twelve men whom Jesus one day called to himself, he called them by name, that they might remain with him and that he might send them out to preach (cf. *Mk* 3:13-19). "Apostle", in fact, is a Greek word meaning "sent", "dispatched". An Apostle is a person who has been given a mandate, he is sent to do something and the Apostles were chosen, called and sent out by Jesus to continue his work, that is to pray - which is the primary job of an apostle - and, second, to proclaim the Gospel. This is important, because when we think of the Apostles we might think that they were only sent out to proclaim the Gospel, to do many good deeds. However, a problem arose in the early times of the Church because of how much the Apostles had to do, and that is why they instituted deacons, so that there would be more time for the Apostles to pray and proclaim the Word of God.

Being an apostle

When we think of the Successors of the Apostles, the bishops - this includes the Pope for he too is a bishop - we must ask ourselves if this successor of the Apostles prays first and then proclaims the Gospel: this is what it means to be an apostle and this is what makes the Church apostolic. Every one of us, if we want to be apostles as I shall explain now, must ask ourselves: do I pray for the salvation of the world? Do I proclaim the Gospel? This is the Church apostolic! It is the constitutive bond that we have with the Apostles. Starting from this I would like to focus briefly on the three meanings of the adjective "apostolic" as it is applied to the Church.

The authority of the Apostles

The Church is apostolic because she is *founded on the preaching and prayer of the Apostles*, on the authority that was entrusted to them by Christ himself. St Paul writes to the Christians of Ephesus: "You are no longer strangers and sojourners, but you are fellow citizens with the saints and members of the household of God, built upon the foundation of the apostles and prophets, Christ

Jesus himself being a cornerstone" (2:19-20); that is, he compares Christians to living stones that form an edifice that is the Church, and this edifice is founded on the Apostles, like columns, and the cornerstone that carries it all is Jesus himself. Without Jesus the Church cannot exist! Jesus is the foundation of the Church, the foundation! The Apostles lived with Jesus, they listened to his words, they shared his life, above all they were witnesses of his Death and Resurrection. Our faith, the Church that Christ willed, is not based on an idea, it is not based on a philosophy, it is based on Christ himself. And the Church is like a plant that over the long centuries has grown, has developed, has borne fruit, yet her roots are planted firmly in him and that fundamental experience of Christ which the Apostles had, chosen and sent out by Jesus, reaching all the way to us. From this little plant to our day: this is how the Church has spread everywhere in the world.

The Church hands on the Apostles' teaching

But let us ask ourselves: how is it possible for us to be connected to that testimony, how could what the Apostles experienced with Jesus, what they heard from him reach us? This is the second meaning of the term "apostolic". *The Catechism of the Catholic Church* states that the Church is apostolic because "with the help of the Spirit dwelling in her, the Church *keeps and hands on* the teaching, the 'good deposit', the salutary words she has heard from the Apostles" (n. 857). Over the centuries, the Church conserves this precious treasure, which is Sacred Scripture, doctrine, the sacraments, the ministry of pastors, so that we can be faithful to Christ and share in his very life. It is like a river coursing through history, developing, irrigating; but running water always comes from a source, and the source is Christ himself: he is the Risen One, he is the Living One, and his words never pass away, for he does not pass, he is alive, he is among us today, he hears us and we speak to him and he listens, he is in our hearts. Jesus is with us today! This is the beauty of the Church: the presence of Jesus Christ among us. Do we ever think about how important this gift that Jesus gave us is, the gift of the Church, where we can meet him? Do we ever think about how it is precisely the Church on her journey through the centuries - despite the difficulties, the problems, the weaknesses, our sins - that transmits to us the authentic message of Christ? She gives us the certainty that what we believe in is really what Christ communicated to us.

The missionary nature of the Church

My final thought: the Church is apostolic because she is *sent to bring the Gospel to all the world*. She continues in history the mission which Jesus entrusted to the Apostles: "Go therefore and make disciples of all nations, baptising them in the name of the Father and of the Son and of the Holy Spirit, teaching them to observe all that I have commanded you; and lo, I am with you always, to the close of the age" (*Mt* 28:19-20). This is what Jesus told us to do! I insist on this missionary aspect, because Christ invites all to "go out" and encounter others, he sends us, he asks us to move in order to spread the joy of the Gospel! Once again let us ask ourselves: are we missionaries by our words, and especially by our Christian life, by our witness? Or are we Christians closed in our hearts and in our churches, sacristy Christians? Are we Christians in name only, who live like pagans? We must ask ourselves these questions, which are not a rebuke. I ask myself as well: what kind of Christian am I, is my witness true?

Rediscovering the Church's apostolic beauty

The Church's roots are in the teaching of the Apostles, the authentic witnesses of Christ, but she looks to the future, she has the firm consciousness of being sent - sent by Jesus - of being missionary, bearing the name of Jesus by her prayer, proclaiming it and testifying to it. A Church that is closed in on herself and in the past, a Church that only sees the little rules of behaviour, of attitude, is a Church that betrays her own identity; a closed Church betrays her own identity! Then, let us rediscover today all the beauty and responsibility of being the Church apostolic! And remember this: the Church is apostolic because we pray - our first duty - and because we proclaim the Gospel by our life and by our words.

Mary, Image of the Church

Continuing our catecheses on the Church, today I would like to look at Mary as the image and model of the Church. I will do so by taking up an expression of the Second Vatican Council. The Constitution *Lumen Gentium* states: "As St Ambrose taught, the Mother of God is a type of the Church in the order of faith, charity, and the perfect union with Christ" (n. 63).

Our Lady is the model of faith

Let us begin with the first aspect, *Mary as the model of faith*. In what sense does Mary represent a model for the Church's faith? Let us think about who the Virgin Mary was: a Jewish girl who was waiting with all her heart for the redemption of her people. But in the heart of the young daughter of Israel there was a secret that even she herself did not yet know: in God's loving plan she was destined to become the Mother of the Redeemer. At the Annunciation, the Messenger of God calls her "full of grace" and reveals this plan to her. Mary answers "yes" and from that moment Mary's faith receives new light: it is concentrated on Jesus, the Son of God, who from her took flesh and in whom all the promises of salvation history are fulfilled. Mary's faith is the fulfilment of Israel's faith, the whole journey, the whole path of that people awaiting redemption is contained in her, and it is in this sense that she is the model of the Church's faith, which has Christ, the incarnation of God's infinite love, as its centre.

Faith in ordinary things

How did Mary live this faith? She lived it out in the simplicity of the thousand daily tasks and worries of every mother, such as providing food, clothing, caring for the house... It was precisely Our Lady's normal life which served as the basis for the unique relationship and profound dialogue which unfolded between her and God, between her and her Son. Mary's "yes", already perfect from the start, grew until the hour of the Cross. There her motherhood opened to embrace every one of us, our lives, so as to guide us to her Son. Mary lived perpetually immersed in the mystery of God-made-man, as his first and perfect disciple, by contemplating all things in her heart in the light of the Holy Spirit, in order to understand and live out the will of God. We can ask ourselves a question: do we allow ourselves to be illumined by the faith of Mary, who is our Mother? Or do we think of her as distant, as someone too different from us? In moments of difficulty, of trial, of darkness, do we look to her as a model of trust in God who always and only desires our good? Let's think about this: perhaps it will do us good to rediscover Mary as the model and figure of the Church in this faith that she possessed!

A model of charity

We come to the second aspect: *Mary as the model of charity*. In what way is Mary a living example of love for the Church? Let us think the readiness she showed toward her cousin Elizabeth. In visiting her, the Virgin Mary brought not only material help - she brought this too - but she also brought Jesus, who was already alive in her womb. Bringing Jesus into that house meant bringing joy, the fulness of joy. Elizabeth and Zechariah were rejoicing at a pregnancy that had seemed impossible at their age, but it was the young Mary who brought them the fulness of joy, the joy which comes from Jesus and from the Holy Spirit, and is expressed by gratuitous charity, by sharing with, helping, and understanding others.

Mary brings her Son to us

Our Lady also wants to bring the great gift of Jesus to us, to us all; and with him she brings us his love, his peace, and his joy. In this, the Church is like Mary: the Church is not a shop, she is not a humanitarian agency, the Church is not an NGO. The Church is sent to bring Christ and his Gospel to all. She does not bring herself - whether small or great, strong or weak, the Church carries Jesus and should be like Mary when she went to visit Elizabeth. What did Mary take to her? Jesus. The Church brings Jesus: this is the centre of the Church, to carry Jesus! If, as a hypothesis, the Church were not to bring Jesus, she would be a dead

Church. The Church must bring Jesus, the love of Jesus, the charity of Jesus.

Learning to love

We have spoken about Mary, about Jesus. What about us? We who are the Church? What kind of love do we bring to others? Is it the love of Jesus that shares, that forgives, that accompanies, or is it a watered-down love, like wine so diluted that it seems like water? Is it a strong love, or a love so weak that it follows the emotions, that it seeks a return, an interested love? Another question: is self-interested love pleasing to Jesus? No, it is not, because love should be freely given, like his is. What are the relationships like in our parishes, in our communities? Do we treat each other like brothers and sisters? Or do we judge one another, do we speak evil of one another, do we just tend our own vegetable patch? Or do we care for one another? These are the questions of charity!

Mary is one with Christ

And briefly, one last aspect: *Mary as the model of union with Christ*. The life of the Holy Virgin was the life of a woman of her people: Mary prayed, she worked, she went to the synagogue... But every action was carried out in perfect union with Jesus. This union finds its culmination on Calvary: here Mary is united to the Son in the martyrdom of her heart and in the offering of his life to the Father for the salvation of humanity. Our Lady shared in the pain of the Son and accepted with him the will of the Father, in that obedience that bears fruit, that grants the true victory over evil and death. The reality Mary teaches us is very beautiful: to always be united with Jesus. We can ask ourselves: do we remember Jesus only when something goes wrong and we are in need, or is ours a constant relation, a deep friendship, even when it means following him on the way of the Cross? Let us ask the Lord to grant us his grace, his strength, so that the model of Mary, Mother of the Church, may be reflected in our lives and in the life of every ecclesial community. So be it!

Sources

This book draws together the Wednesday Audience Catecheses of Pope Francis given in St Peter's Square between 22nd May and 23rd October 2013.

Introduction: 22nd May

The Church as the Family of God: 29th May

The People of God: 12th June

The Body of Christ: 19th June

The Temple: 26th June

The Church Our Mother: 11th September

Mother Church Again: 18th September

The Church is One: 25th September

The Church is Holy: 2nd October

The Church is Catholic: 9th October

The Church is Apostolic: 16th October

Mary, Image of the Church: 23rd October